Y0-DKM-657

Liberty Plays Her Part

A Poetry Collection of Modern Times

by

INGRID E. BRIDGES

LIFE TO LEGACY

Liberty Plays Her Part:
A Poetry Collection of Modern Times
by Ingrid E. Bridges, Copyright © 2019

ISBN-13: 978-1-947288-46-1
ISBN-10: 1-947288-46-6

All rights reserved solely by the author under international Copyright Law. Except where designated, the author certifies that all contents are original and do not infringe upon the legal rights of any other person or work. No part of this book may be reproduced in any form without the expressed written permission of the publisher.

Cover design by: Legacy Design
                   legacydesigninc@gmail.com

Printed in the United States

10 9 8 7 6 5 4 3 2 1

Published by:
Life To Legacy, LLC
P.O. Box 1239
Matteson IL 60443
www.Life2Legacy.com
877-267-7477
www.life2legacy.com

Table of Contents

Table of Contents

<u>Dedication</u>

To my husband, Harry and my son, Brian for believing in me.

Liberty Plans Her Part

Liberty called her friends,
even,
her foes to a dance,
to laugh,
to be merry,
to unite nations
far and near.

Liberty called them all
to befriend one another,
to open bitter arms wide,
to those across the land.

She, ask them to join her
in welcoming
lost souls, lost nations,
lost words to her yard of freedom,
where her table of equality and love
offers many fruits to enjoy.

They sat down.
First bewildered,
secondly uncertain,
with distorted reasons in their hearts.

Liberty took notes as
they argued about truth,
argued about unfairness,
argued over hate and gave personal greed the door.

Liberty listened closely as
tradition began settling old opinions.

Together like old pals,
the obliged watched a brilliant sunrise,
the smitten hid from an oozing sunset.

Like pigs in heat,
they ate rich cake,
broke holy bread,
drank red foreign wine
and then slept hard.

Liberty who never sleeps,
soaked up their horrible dreams
and dissected their vicious thoughts.

Liberty secretly
excused their nightmares,
disrupted their plots,
hid their personal agendas,
photographed their heart strings,
and removed selfishness motives
impostered as good.

Morning came late,
horridly like a ghost.
They departed
unsure of their decisions,
but,
remembering a reluctant truce.
Liberty watched as centuries passed by,
as generations became anew.

Colors were then charted as few,
different cultures were there too,

asking "who rules the land of the free?"
As the year 2000 painted America's calendars, old shadows
saw a new day birth enlightenment
upon once, stormy seas.

A rainbow of joyous friends, again, aligned her shores,
as
liberty open her vast doors
to all
tall,
blond,
black,
brown,
red and white, too.

Liberty ask those attending her dance
are any rebuttals among you...
if so,
please stand up and show your new face
and
we all will watch you sleep well.

An Unfinished Tale Won't Die

Hollowed be the name
of the Black man,
taken from his inheritance,
where unlimited resources ride free.

Taken to an arctic land called America -
a new land,
a strange place,
where souls are said to run free.

But not for the Black man.

Who runs scared in this strange place,
Where his fears raise no brows,
being not welcomed, yet he was invited.

But woe unto the pale face
and woe unto he,
who defiled a heritage,
stolen,
sold never to be set free again.

Yet glory was watching,
yes,
glory,
who sent a man,
a Black man, to reclaim,
not only a name but a lost kingdom dying within.

A man named Dr. Martin Luther King, Jr.,
born on a cold day,
under a blazing red sun.

King,
a name of strength or rule,
who God anointed in the womb,
as a deliverer of a tribe,
in a nation running free.

There, he stood on a mountain,
justifying, clarifying God's rule.

First they stopped,
then they,
the pale faced, who frowned,

spitted,
debated,
laughing at his civil ways of thinking, listened.

For a people once told they had no control
nor place or thoughts.

This man, named King, heard a voice say

"Nigger no more,
slave boy no more,
but my beautiful colored one."
"You, my chosen species, carry out my promises,
save my people,
all the red,
the black,
the yellow,
the white to be free."

Free, I say,
free in soul,
insight,
free to love,
to laugh,
to delight,

where they touch and cry in joy.
Small in height,
he fought with might,
a battle over run by hate,
by whites.

Listening closely to the sirens of a
shackled nation, tied, dyed,
hung to rot in the morning sun.

King heard His Father in Heaven say

> *"Move up, step forward win this chess game*
> *of endearing life."*
> *"It's time to speak,*
> *to talk with hope. "*
> *"Be bold,*
> *hold no tears back,*
> *and tell the real story of freedom,*
> *of love."*

Climbing dusty mountains was no tale,
for his fathers,
for his mothers,
remembering the dark living hell,

where human souls were
bought, sold and killed.

Across America's white steps,
where fathers founded rest.
King rose,
telling his story of freedom.

King, standing as the undebatable icon,
wisdom teaching southern preacher,
playing a constant drum.

Oh, what significance is the beat,
they all march too,
one by one on their feet,
hoping to reach a promised land where glory
awaits and the drum beats on.

This poem is inspired by a statement spoken by the late
Dr. Martin Luther King Jr., in 1968, which reads:

*"It is not only poverty that torments the Negro; it is the fact of poverty
amid plenty. It is a misery generated by the gulf between the affluence
he sees in the mass media and the deprivation he experiences in his
everyday life."*

Fifty Reasons To Count

Only once in a lifetime we may get a chance
to remember years past with ease.

When childlike behaviors are long gone,
dreams once dreamt are now half fulfilled,
long to do list,
still remaining undone.

And yet we still laugh.

Knowing our golden years have arrive on time,
that our best years are awaiting us across life's
amazing shores, somewhere, unknown.

We learn to no longer count our days,
nor the years,
that are long gone,
forgotten,
once hidden
or lost.

Maybe once or twice
we count
candles on our birthday cakes,
fingers on hands and toes we depend on each day.

After five decades,
looking out over ageless waters from cruise ships,
pulling away from yesterday's bay
we can begin, again.

Counting
waves dancing on seas,
eggs sleeping on ripen figs,
where loose pennies once fell in the grass.

By grace,
we arrived safely at
a place never seen before,
with fifty new reasons to compare,
life's toil,
life's laughter,
life's roller coaster rides,
under star gazed nights with someone new.

Again we count the years.

An Inherited Ride Not for Sale!

Family,
a one-way ticket with no returns.

A gift,
a curse,
a symbol of unselfish love.

A brother, a mother, a sister, a father,
if lucky it's grandparents and great grand-parents,
living,
thriving,
talking,
crying,
shouting,
sometimes complaining.

It's their sign of loving you,
what's given is not earned,
what inherited is not earned.

The ticket is free, no charge.
On that journey
habits are formed.

Patterns are formed and
passed on.

Family albums are saved where old
memories can be either
good or bad.

Every holiday tells the story,
how families dwell,
how families die

Is family a network of different people making choices -
upon the heart-strings of those
who love, and those, who hate?

Someone moves forward as a knight
on the chessboard of life,
in love, the rest will follow.

In hate, some will crumble,
leaving footprints of despair.

Family is the strong merchant who pays the bills,
tithes and children's tuitions on time.

And family could be a locked door with no key;
saying no more chances, the boardwalks full.

By then,   ,
window sills look beautiful from the outside
as the homeless look in.

As grandma's baking good whistle their forgotten name.

As we reflect...
family stands for those meaningful
moments spent on God's good earth together;
like two or more standing at the gate of
expectation.

Standing strong when the wind blows,
Standing strong not weak when the bow breaks,

yet they stand together, united, as one.

Family invites the defeated ones' home
allowing them to rest – to regroup
never saying no when hard times hit,
giving love if nothing else.

Family is that love,
family is that strength,
family is all that contains unity – despite
the tides that wash upon the vast shores of life.

Hurting souls should know that.
Homeless ones should know that.
Family should encourage that.

Build not tear down,
greet not defeat,
offer cheer not fear.

For family is a ride only some are rewarded,
as a one – way journey, singing a funny song.

Fee Foe, Me

The foe once entertained
smiled like me,
dined at fancy places with me,
bought my child some milk,
took my son to baseball practice,
washed my soiled clothing when I was too sick to
lift my head.

My foe was so close to me,
painting my shadow, a new color to attain its luck.

Often smelling like a pink rose in spring.

One day I saw a reflection of my foe in the pond
near the park. I noticed no other man or woman,
instead I saw me.

A pitiful shimmer of the person I once was.
I saw a mean hateful person,
never happy with my deeds,
always critical of my work, my gifts, my worth.

I saw for the first time in years,
my enemy I carried around like a backpack,
like a human organ,
like a tooth that bites porterhouse steak
steadily devouring me way.

Then the giant in me,
rose up, grew up,
became strong, became wise,
stood for the first time in life.

Realizing the window was open wide,
where a river over flowing with milk, and honey
and candy too,
was my pathway.

Now I am smiling at others, helping others,
knowing I broke the six-year curse of me, me, me
and my foe lived no more.

With Loving You

Because I sought higher ground,
a silent refuge spoke my name.

Buried deep within,
where souls dance with wolves,
where friends kiss fairies,
where love says, hello.

Being in love,
began a soft melody in my heart.

Afternoons fly by,
nights seem too short,
even Saturdays turned their faces,
toward Sunday morning too soon.

Higher ground seems all right this time,
with loving you.

Sweet Purpose

Caramel chocolate sundaes, strawberry shortcakes,
peanut butter cookies, ice cold creamy milk,
tell sweet stories like water falling from Niagara's
wall.

Never doubt a civil purpose,
never second guess a justified truth.

If only,
bell captains, blew golden whistles
life guards, saved all lives,
blues music poured out pure joy,
there would be sweet desserts,
sweet justice,
sweet equality,
everywhere,
for everyone.

My Heart Surrenders All

Laying here in bondage,
bound by bars with
heavy locks.

Chose a rough road,
even graduated many times,
from schools of bitter fights and
hard knocks.

Maybe our creator hears me or hears me not,
at the game of have and have nots.

Now looking out at the world through a keyhole in
a cell, as a recess yard calls my name, but, I hear
not.

My heart turned over many times,
asking forgiveness if anyone could hear.

Finally,
smelling willows in the southern air,
far, far away from a place called home,
reminds me of urban kids,
playing my old song.

Now, I have learned to surrender all.

Mozart Just For Me

These legs may not run like they use too,
hands don't grasp nor twist jars like they once did
but,
I am alive,
and well, I profess.

These wrinkles across my brow are more intense,
but my smile is as bright as decades ago in my
youth.

My ole friend remembers me,
my grocer knows me too,
the post man, still, says hello,
when no one in the entire world has a good word
to throw my way.

Yet I live,
vibrant,
fervent,
ready, dressed to kill as the symphony plays Mozart
just for me.

Friendly Smiles, Beware

Jealousy,
a piercing eye,
a sorrowful gesture,
a cheap way out,
a defacing example,
a coward's cry,
a fleeting foe's ammunition.

Jealousy,
a silly grin,
a faceless treason,
a small man's armor,
a bruised ego gone mad,
a rich person's only vice,
a poor man's sorrow.

Jealousy,
an evil person's growl,
a short man heated argument with a tall one,
a fatherless child's defense,
a sibling's joy ride,
a boss with no future.

Jealousy,
a co-workers venom,
a spider's web,
the devil's shovel,
an ex-lovers treasure chest,
a spiraling, crowded road.

Jealousy,
a child's lesson,
a close friend 's quiet hate,
a place where fools abide,
quietly,
an enemy's mirror on a wall.

Hello My Friend, Good Bye

Our lives, became united on perfected paths,
where we once wondered.

Moving along God's profound highways,
often aloof
yet, before we ran,
we walked,
we went.

Often, we ventured,
among the greatest,
witnessed their reign together,
enjoying their triumph.

We witnessed splendor within king's corridors,
even sat upon polished thrones at their unawares,
in marble palaces, where we dreamed deep, day
dreams.

And each important hand we shook,
was followed by an innocent laugh,
like a funny girl's first dance.

Our pretty faces were aglow with youth,
back then,

our shining hours were many.
Forsaking no one,
we enjoyed life's unexpected delights.

Every morning sunrise, we promise to set fine
tables preparing to harness the changing winds of
time.

Aging brows, however turned gray,
we now recollect life's memories.

Memories of intrigue,
adventure,
and
sometimes sorrow,
still we held on tight.

And yet we know time has limited access
for our life journey
soon will return to its beginning.

Where fools never rise,
and
the road ahead says boldly, hello
to my familiar friend,
good - bye.

In His Likeness, They Dare Not

He walked quietly,
despite an illuminating stature.

Some wondered His cause,
like those before the Cherokee nation.

His arrival,
never spoken when seen
between cherry wood
and applewood trees.

He waltzed among curious marsh meadows,
His heartbeat humming, softly,
when mountains began playing
an echo of old Indian flutes once in awe,
ants say, He giggled, just a bit.

Heard by hooting owls at midnight,
crickets hid under forgotten rocks,
together, unified, they silently welcomed Him.

Like ages ago,
they recall His friendly whisper,
blowing in an ancient wind.

Enchanting,
spell bounding is His elegance,
absorbed for miles by grass standing
dirty green.

Brooks suddenly,
turned directions at His glance,
changing tunes in mid-stream.

Called early by His maker,
never fearing not one command.

His walk was soon heard
even by caterpillars transforming
on skinny branches.

Beetles sleeping underneath,
His earth's floor,
woke up early

as howling wolves stopped, in their,
tracks at His mention,
still,
in the night, placidly He walks.

Unlike human creatures of the earth,
His purpose,
His reign,
would last forever, even His silhouette,
aglow.

Mending, blending
in mother earth's silent breeze.

Sunsets became His armor bearers,
moon lit skies bowed down,
even powder blue skies gave Him homage, His due.

Like winter,
like spring,
they awaited His glory,
knowing of Him through the years.

Mountains of Wyoming still remain His
amazement,
Niagara Falls, His greatest release,
Grand Canyon, His melting pot,
Yosemite a constant wonder, while
Yellowstone caves offers a personal song.

All creation,
all living behind the stars unite,
applauding His magnificence,
not one, challenging His love for them all.

His soft walk,
always being felt in a gentle breeze,
never speaking a single word,
no not one.

And,
His presence,
relentlessly,
without a human gesture,
still,
His illumination, His presence,
heals them all.

Love Him, Still

Tell him,
tell him you love him,
you adore him.

Hug him,
really hug him,
spoil him,
cook for him,
prepare his favorite dish!

Kiss him,
lay with him
lay on him,
rock him no matter the time of day.

Think of him,
tell him,
you
love him, still.

Cry with him
cry for him,
support him,
cheer him on.

Disagree with him.
yet strengthen him.

Walk with him,
run with him
smell him,
smell the air he breathes.

Dream big dreams with him,
see that he achieves
his dreams or least try...

Greet him no matter the hour,
meet him whenever time allows,
surprise him anytime...but
tell him,
you love him still...

A Last Chance

Stand your ground
love her,
but don't abuse,
nor abandon her.

Listen to her woes,
her stories,
her shortcomings.

Applaud her achievements with a kiss!

Sweeten her when bitterness
knocks at the shores of those dreams
you both, share.

Be bigger in her shadows,
know you are a leader of your journey
together.

Tell her she's included,
knowing that she'll be yours, forever

remind her the world will not break your bond.

Take her for a ride,
a trip,
a train ride
and just talk.

Be her victor,
be her winner,
be her strong tower of strength that
knights and shining armors were made of long
ago.

Treat her as your most prized gift
holding her tight,
holding her close like your first time together.

.

Thirst

Sacred wisdom always quenches those who thirst...

Walk With A New Ease

No longer bound by negative reports,
dark statistics, for today I walk.

For the very first time
I walk, and I see clearly.

I see a rainbow around me
I see a sky so blue above my head
I see rivers of possibility in every step I take
I notice tall buildings are hovering around about me.

Like never before
I see pretty babies in strollers, laughing
I see old men with canes, dancing
I see trees with green leaves,
some with new buds,
some with fruit on their vines.

I am so glad I took this walk,
chose common places to roam,
where paths were once said, forbidden.

I see what probably has always been
awaiting me, for now I walk with ease.

Universe In Black

Black like me,
a purely defined metal, stubbornly dossed without
stain, made under pressure.

Born out of mountains climbed as midnight
amusement over a dancing cold lake,
where taunting waves lay suspiciously under sunlit
mornings,
darkness standing tall, not weak.

A chorus of sacred themes heard weeping,
outstretched hands of wonderment applaud,
just scraps found in torrid rain, where muddy marsh
lands, where willows once grew beautifully wild.

Black like me, are these hungry, tired, bones and
feet,
waiting on road sides where no concrete, nor
cement meet.
No more songs moan or groan near melting roots
of old trees.

Without humor, but a familiar joy aglow
still, so tired from a long, long journey,
tired from relentless strangers of bruised love,
fevered by pain pouring upon old bones,
still cold heading six feet deep.

Laid bones,
our grandmothers' bones,
our father's father back bones,
his father's back bones, too.

Black like me are rich soiled terrains,
dark winter's nights,
old bits of old coal from a forgotten mine, slick
long hair, coarse too,
grizzly bears in quiet woods running from a blazing
sun at noon.

We have no troubles with other men,
our tiredness is too worn,
our minds, half worn too,
that our dreams, left early to hide somewhere safe,
like a grave buried so deep in mother earth,
where our ancestors' dreams are there...kept

hidden in the Blackness.

Black like me
are hands so rough,
dried from sun drenched labor,
always picking cotton in fields where
black faces appear dark blue.

Days are long tired,
like grandfather's grandfather would say,
too weary, too broke down to say
"how do you do."

Wearing many hues,
brilliantly brown,
exquisitely bronze,
profoundly golden,
marvelously Black,

Born straight from Heaven
no blue eyes,
no deep green eyes,
no lavender hues to sale,
just brown eyed

kindly playing the fool to survive a master's lashes.

Black, like me are sounds heard from zebra piano
keys, serenading soil under tall aging oak trees,
nurturing tomorrow's shady places,
where all the dirty foes run to hide,
a midnight's whisper,
before an early morning dew leaf
her handkerchief upon the stones of old.

Like stargazing skies,
standing in the mist,
kinfolk dreams play ole' spiritual songs,
songs that whisper secret prayers.
Remembering heart's desires
traveling in sync where a rumored milky way once
glowed.

Beautifully made,
brilliantly dancing,
laughing far above the
clouds where God says otherwise,
far, far, far away,

from a distance cloud,
yes, they lay still being unseen,
but Black like me!

Far Away Places

Beautifully black like me are far away places, like
Africa,
Egypt,
Iran,
Iraq,
and Libya too.

Where symbols of God's chosen are painted in
dazzling shades,
of Black, brown, golden blue.

Mirrors depicting many like me, like them, like
you.
Black presidents
Black leaders
Black advocates
Black diamonds
Black oil buried under blood driven dust
disguised as dirty streams dead over time.

Black faces
are there too,
seeking freedom.
Freedom to laugh,

freedom to run,
freedom to speak,
freedom to be,
beautifully free,
beautifully Black,
like me.

Morning Sun Shine

Last night buried its face,
this morning's dashing sunshine reminds me of it.

This small room I slept in last night is different
now,
the door way leading to the outside world, today
appears somehow much larger.

The street I live on,
is finally quieter,
the world appears
safer, too.

What a difference a few little hours can make,
when the world keeps a space on the Boardwalk.

A Last Chance

Stand your ground
love her but don't abuse her,
nor abandon her.

Listen to her woes,
her stories,
her shortcomings.

Applaud her achievements with a hug, with a kiss,
Sweeten her inside when bitterness
knocks at the shores of those timeless dreams
you both shares.

Be bigger in her shadows,
know you are the leader of your destiny
together.

Tell her she's included on your journey,
Tell she'll be yours, forever,
remind her the world's trickery
will not break your bond.

Take her for a ride,
on a trip,
a train ride
and just talk, even whisper something new.

Be her victor,
be her winner,
be her strong tower of strength that
knights and shining armors are made of.

Treat as your most prized gift
and hold her tight,
and hold her close
like your first time together.

What If...

What if Abraham Lincoln
never thought of
freeing America's slaves, just what if he said "no"?

What if Dr. Martin Luther King Jr.,
stood for violence, spoke on hate,
never stood for peace,
human rights, civil rights,
what if...
he thought otherwise?

What if psychics, stargazers and warlocks
ruled the land,
designed one's life path,
decided life's journey,
just, what if?

What if leaders were led by spoilers,
cheated the defeated,
beat down the worn, what if?

What if giving birth was a mandate,
everyone,
every man,
every woman,
had to conceive no matter what, what if?

What if mother earth was no longer a place? but a
day dream on a planet with no light... just what if?

What if all souls had no choice?
but to live forever and ever and ever wandering
through eternity with no resting place, what if?

What if every face shared the same shade? every
person had the same identity...what if?

What if the rich became broke?
being the same class
was everyone's fate?

Would there be any wars? What if?
What if?
What if?

What if truth was the only way to exist, and cheating,
lying and double mindedness was a crime of
fatal punishment, no second chances...what if?

What if everything living had only one purpose,
leaving no wars to be fought, nor voices to be heard,
nor leaders to make laws to be broken...just what if?

What if there was no currency, no common exchange?
everything in the land was free in abundance...what if?

What if water, sodium, sulfur, oxygen and rich
soil of the earth dried up, leaving famine and
desolation for everyone around the world,
simultaneously...what if?

What if there were no fathers?
only mothers,
only mothers
only mothers reproducing by machines, what if?
and there were no men, no males....
What if?

What if God decided to reconstruct humanity all
together?
Tomorrow, leaving no stone unturned,
leaving only insects to exist...what if?

What if each day began with darkness?
Never giving humanity light, sunshine,
maybe on holidays…what if?

What if God had not given the world
His only begotten Son, to save the world from themselves,
from old sin, new sin and all sins,
just what if?

No Hands On My Clock

Time never over sleeps,
never runs out,
never arrives too early,
always shows up.
When the world
close its eyes... time stays awake

Fields of Color
(Red Planet)

Humanity, sought a better environment
where
all races,
all colors,
all shades,
all cultures of people,
finally, are living side by side,
road after road,
shack by shack,
house by house,
working, breathing, surviving.
But are they really living?

The new neighbors say they just escaped
to another reality where nothingness is a
permanent playmate.

A Timeless Wonder

Time a questionable wonder,
wasted,
bought,
spent,
purchased,
given,
cherished,
used wisely for some.

Time never waits,
Time never waste away,
Time hits and runs,

Punctual,
often telling what gives,
what does not.

Lends no more time,
but sometimes, if luck is on your side.

When Winter Stops
by...Wedding Bells

Thwarted thorns,
broken branches,
falling leaves
russet, red, brown, and maroon,
wave goodbye to summer's end.

Squirrel's prepare their warm nest,
birds gather their best,
autumn winds spend short days
playing a symphony of new songs,
welcoming cold breezes back home.

Winter always says' hello,
laughing,
bringing snow falls
big snow falls
that are deep
saluting cold and chilly nights.
Days make love,

lover's make love too
under dusk dark skies,
until midnight skies,
shine bright.

Another cold night,
another windy cold night,
where wind, rain, snow and sleet
join hands.

Lovers get closer,
lovers grow closer,
before you know it,
a new shining engagement ring
and they all become one,
sounds like a June wedding
is near,
under sunlit rays,
powder blue skies
holding long awaited hands,
saying "I love you."

So Long, Too Soon

One decade has now past.
Life's moving forward, placidly,
often greeted by carefree sunshines...
violent rains, barrels of unexpected snowfalls.

And somehow.
Us, who have never forgotten.
Our memories of broken dreams lost too soon,
in so many young lives,
are fresh, vibrant as a powder blue summer sky.

We remember them all,
their voices heard in an echo,
their smiles dancing on a rainbow,
the last song they heard,
still we hear it too.

The Prize of Paradise

Your endless mesmerizing touch,
has led me into your spellbinding love nest.

Fever lies inside my body as you
come,
and,
when you go.

I stay awake through the dark,
mysterious nights,
holding on to your last good bye...

Truly I have your love...
yes,
endlessly in my dreams.

As I awake to the morning sun
awaiting your moist lips
upon my breast.

I suddenly cry with joy
a dash of joy

severe ecstasy,
yearns to see you again.

If your love for me would end,
my heart would be shattered like a broken mirror,
torn like a silk imported sheet
and
there
would be my tombstone.

My life would be forever cold,
frozen like winter's mean face,
without warmth,
without you my dear.

Although, grace,
and,
fate,
has been good to me,
and you are here.

Now
standing tall in my arms,
thirsting for my body to hold yours,

tighter and tighter,
and,
my sensuality,
my loins are interlocking
your masculine touch,
and all my deepest desires are becoming true.

I never stop believing,
my faith never lied,
you my darling are my prize,
and I won,
and will keep winning,
as long as your love keeps loving me.

Let Them Eat

Babies on every side of my tiny table.
Some small, some not so tall,
a big boy who like raisin toast and jam.

Maybe there will not be enough food
to feed them all.

Well,
like Mama would do,
I won't eat.

But, my babies will, eat
food, I mean.

Built By the Best

Mothers,
a brilliant pattern,
uncarved by man.

The first face,
saw close,
saw near.
A mother,
a witness,
a biological wonder,
given as a gift by God's mighty hand.

Mothers,
a divine ingredient,
humanity's complex puzzle,
called after man.

Witness to His source of new beginnings,
equipped early within the hidden palace,
the chamber,
the womb,
where human wonders begin to rumble.
Built to never breakdown,
no, she never will.

Kangaroo Green

Soldier boy, who are you?
Dressed in green berets,
dark green kangaroo.

Eating well at times,
side by side,
but a boy wanting to lead,
like you, stands watching you, too.

Sergeant says "Give him 20,
give him 50 lashes,
you thought,
you could
beat him at his own game of cards.

Don't shoot the children,
when they run behind bushes,
behind trees.
Don't shoot their mother's like old worn men do.
Save the world,
save a country,
soldier boy dressed in disguised blue.

Are you really a soldier representing the red, the white, the blue?

Too many are dying,
even your friends,
young
bright, astute too.

Fighting a war?
While a nation, crying out for Benjamins,
Washington's, Grants too.

Forefathers,
found war
a game,
a plot,
a rule,
are you one of them, roaming in a trance?

Like men,
blinded by an imaginary truth.

Don't kill them,
the children, I mean,
they are hungry, eating leaves,
dirt,
garbage,

with scared mothers,
on an island of an innocent few.

Rumors of wars are now truths,
Although the Bible speaks of rumors the battle is
not yours, the Bible also says, it's the Lord.

Soldier boy,
dressed in green berets,
smiling,
shyly
like green kangaroos,
whose are you?"

Walk With Me

No longer bound by negative reports,
prognostics,
statistics, today I walk.

For the very first time
I walk free.

I see a rainbow around me,

I see a sky so blue above my head,

I see rivers of possibility in every step I take

I notice tall buildings are hovering around about me.

Like never, before,

I see pretty babies in strollers, laughing
I see old men with canes, dancing,
I see trees with deep green leaves,
some with new buds,
some with fruit on their vines.

I am so glad I took this walk,
chose common places to roam,
where paths were once said, forbidden.
I see what probably has always been
awaiting me,
as I walk with ease.

Rest Stop

The day traveled faster than most,
maybe,
the day's sun rose to early, and
yesterday,
the sun set too late.

After dawn,
a blue moon crossed over my life,
probably too quickly,
leaving me to count a number
of blazing stars
circling heaven's door.

Although dizzy from God's amazement,
I took time to see over a road across the way,
I see now,
rest was calling me to reflect.

Now I arise
determined
to adore another day,
where life lends me a caravan of possibilities,
created personally,
abundantly,
without compromise, or regret.

Egg No Longer On My Face

The sun the weatherman spoke about is now
shining in my life.

The closer I get to making my bed,
taking my morning shower,
preparing my burnt toast,
a new wave can flow into my future.

My sunny side egg is ready, and I am eating it all.

ABOUT THE AUTHOR

JOURNALIST, INGRID E. BRIDGES, for over two decades, is known in Chicago circles as a profound writer with hundreds of powerfully moving articles in the Chicago Defender Newspaper, Chicago Sun-Times, N'Digo Mega paper and Ink Pages.

As one of Chicago's award-winning prized writers and orators of spiritual and interfaith issues. She's featured in numerous books and publications including "Who's Who of Chicago" as a legendary writer and "Spirit-Filled Journey" daily devotional.

Currently, she's co-producer, writer and host of the "According To Ingrid" talk show on CAN–TV, cable network, where Bridges expounds about spirituality on a global scale. The show's topics include everything from "The Mayan Calendar Prophecies of 2012" to "Worldwide Takeover of Islam" to "The War between Religion & Politics." Over a million viewers across Chicago land tune into her show since 2010.

Bridges knack for writing began as a curious youngster wanting to appease her peers in high school as the only Black to serve on student council. It worked, due to her savvy choice of animated skits and plots in her prose. She began writing poetry at the age of 12, but professionally her works started to flourish when the religion section of the Chicago Defender Newspaper was a simple one-page listing.

However, after Bridges took the reins as an editor/writer, the daily newspaper's religion listing became a booming, six-page animated spirit-filled section depicting the rich culture of African American religion and worldwide spirituality. She interviewed movie stars, mainstream, and worldwide religious leaders and wrote hard news and the Life Times section, giving her a chance to explore the sciences, news and personal profiles of everyday people.

When the late Cardinal Joseph Bernadine of the Chicago Catholic Archdiocese, took ill, the news department at the Chicago Defender didn't cover it, but Bridges did. Her professional works include one-on-one interviews with such greats as Tiger Woods, Bruce Willis, Dalai Lama, Ambassador Andrew Young, Oprah Winfrey, Mayo Angelo, Bishop T.D. Jakes, Stedman Graham, Bernie Mac, Minister Louis Farrakhan, Cardinal Francis George, Father Michael Pfleger, and hundreds of others in politics, law, and the arts. She holds over 50 awards and citations for her works as a Journalist.

Bridges expertise in ecumenical and interfaith matters, became a household name in religious and political circles, allowing her to serve in a much big arena politics. She served as the liaison to Chicago's Mayor, Richard M. Daley for 16 years, where she worked in the Mayor's Office as a Special Aid to the Faith & African American Community. Working in numerous capacities, mainly in social, civic and ecumenical circles with senators, congressmen, and (then) with Senator, Barack Obama. Officially speaking on behalf of the Mayor before leaders of the interfaith community–African American, Jewish, Buddhist, and Muslim–to build capacity, and enhance relationships within the entire ecumenical community. Bridges was designated to create and write the first "Youth Resource Guide" ever published by the City of Chicago.

Currently, her mission to create, inform and entertain the masses continues in a sea of diverse books known to inspire and uplift those who read her prose. She is also working on completing "Church Lady" about her journey as a reporter in Chicago's huge religious community.

Among her latest literary works is a book entitled, "Just Speak It" (God is listening) depicts what happens when a person chooses to change their course in life toward empowerment and renewed self-esteem. A quick read.

ABOUT THE PUBLISHER

Let us bring your story to life! With Life to Legacy, we offer the following publishing services: manuscript development, editing, transcription services, ghostwriting, cover design, copyright services, ISBN assignment, worldwide distribution, and eBook production and distribution.

Throughout the entire production process, you maintain control over your project. We also specialize in family history books, so you can leave a written legacy for your children, grandchildren, and others. You put your story in our hands, and we'll bring it to literary life! We have several publishing packages to meet all your publishing needs.

Call us at: 877-267-7477, or you can also send e-mail to: Life2Legacybooks@att.net. Please visit our Web site:

www.Life2Legacy.com

CPSIA information can be obtained
at www.ICGtesting.com
Printed in the USA
FFHW020754010419
51323462-56812FF

9 781947 288461